...the world, sharing with travellers a wealth of experience and a passion for travel.

Rely on Thomas Cook as your travelling companion on your next trip and benefit from our unique heritage.

Thomas Cook **pocket** guides

DUNDEE

Thomas Cook

Written by Robin Gauldie

Published by Thomas Cook Publishing
A division of Thomas Cook Tour Operations Limited
Company registration no. 3772199 England
The Thomas Cook Business Park, Unit 9, Coningsby Road,
Peterborough PE3 8SB, United Kingdom
Email: books@thomascook.com, Tel: +44 (0) 1733 416477
www.thomascookpublishing.com

Produced by Cambridge Publishing Management Limited
Burr Elm Court, Main Street, Caldecote CB23 7NU
www.cambridgepm.co.uk

ISBN: 978-1-84848-489-4

First edition © 2011 Thomas Cook Publishing
Text © Thomas Cook Publishing
Cartography supplied by Redmoor Design, Tavistock, Devon
Map data © OpenStreetMap contributors CC-BY-SA, www.openstreetmap.org,
www.creativecommons.org

Series Editor: Karen Beaulah
Production/DTP: Steven Collins

Printed and bound in Spain by GraphyCems

Cover photography © Scottish Viewpoint/Alamy

All rights reserved. No part of this publication may be reproduced, stored in
a retrieval system or transmitted, in any form or by any means, electronic,
mechanical, recording or otherwise, in any part of the world, without prior
permission of the publisher. Requests for permission should be made to the
publisher at the above address.

Although every care has been taken in compiling this publication, and the contents
are believed to be correct at the time of printing, Thomas Cook Tour Operations
Limited cannot accept any responsibility for errors or omissions, however caused,
or for changes in details given in the guidebook, or for the consequences of any
reliance on the information provided. Descriptions and assessments are based on
the author's views and experiences when writing and do not necessarily represent
those of Thomas Cook Tour Operations Limited.

CONTENTS

SYMBOLS KEY

The following symbols are used throughout this book:

ⓐ address **ⓣ** telephone **ⓦ** website address **ⓔ** email
ⓛ opening times **Ⓝ** public transport connections **ⓘ** important

The following symbols are used on the maps:

ⓘ information office   ▧ point of interest
✈ airport   ⭕ city
✚ hospital   ◯ large town
⛊ police station   ○ small town
▱ bus station   = motorway
▤ railway station   — main road
ⓣ tram   minor road
✝ cathedral   — railway
✉ post office
⬛ shopping
❶ numbers denote featured cafés, restaurants & venues

PRICE CATEGORIES
The ratings below indicate average price rates for a double
room per night, including breakfast:
£ under £75 **££** £75–100 **£££** over £100
The typical cost for a three-course meal without drinks
is as follows:
£ under £15 **££** £15–25 **£££** over £25

◗ *The Tay Rail Bridge*

INTRODUCING
Dundee

Introduction

Dundee is Scotland's Cinderella city. It has never had Glasgow's brash cockiness, nor shared Edinburgh's effortless superiority, and in the 1970s it missed out on the big money when Aberdeen was chosen over Dundee as Scotland's oil industry capital. Visitors are often surprised to discover that although this is a city with a history as long as any of its rivals, there are very few visible remnants of the city's medieval past, or even of its recent history. But Dundee is a city with an amazing talent for reinventing itself, and that talent has never been more evident than in the 21st century. Over the last two decades, the city has become a centre of excellence for everything from cutting-edge medical research to equally adventurous digital game design. It's now one of the top choices for students looking for a university city that combines world-class tertiary education with outstanding nightlife and leisure activities. Dundee is increasingly recognised, too, as a great base for exploring a hinterland that combines wide-open wilderness, myriad open-air activities and a tremendous heritage that spans more than 2,000 years.

Dundee came of age during the Industrial Revolution of the 19th century, and in many ways it still shows the scars of more than a century of economic boom and bust. At first sight, on arrival by rail or air, its post-industrial waterfront is not the most charming of vistas. But no city in Scotland can rival the views from within the city looking out. Head for the top of the Dundee Law, the hill that dominates the city skyline, for a panorama that sweeps from the Sidlaw hills and the distant peaks of the

Cairngorms to the open North Sea, and across the miles-wide silver waters of the Firth of Tay to the hills of Fife and upstream to Perth. This is the city that brought the world cartoon character Desperate Dan, poet William McGonagall and pop band Deacon Blue and built the ships that took whalers and explorers to the ends of the earth. Now, in the 21st century, Dundee is more than ever a city of many discoveries.

🔺 *Desperate Dan statue, City Square*

When to go

Dundee is Scotland's only south-facing major city, and it claims to be the sunniest city in Scotland. That said, the winters can still be cold and damp and rain is a possibility even in summer, so waterproof footwear and rainwear are essential items at any time of year. The best time to visit is generally between June and September, with the added advantage that Scotland has far more daylight than England during the summer – in midsummer it doesn't start to get dark until after 10pm. The downside is that in midwinter there are fewer than seven hours of full daylight. Summer daytime temperatures range between 16°C (61°F) and 23°C (73°F) in July and August (the warmest months of the year), while 0°C–7°C (32°F–45°F) is the average in January, the coldest month.

Accommodation is not usually hard to find in Dundee at any time of year, but it is worth bearing in mind that the city is conveniently located between two world-class golfing destinations. Neither Carnoustie nor St Andrews is oversupplied with hotel rooms, so when either of them hosts a major golf tournament, Dundee takes the accommodation overspill and upmarket hotel rooms can be hard to find.

Dundee has a lively calendar of annual events and festivals. The **Dundee Literary Festival** (ⓦ www.literarydundee.co.uk) hosts a number of acclaimed authors from around the world in June, while in September the **Flower and Food Festival** is exactly that – a three-day event featuring guest chefs and competitions ranging from baking to flower arranging (ⓦ www.dundeeflowerandfoodfestival.com). In October feet start tapping to the sounds of Scottish folk fiddlers in the **Fest 'n' Furious festival** (ⓦ www.festnfurious.com) and music fills the city again in November at the highly popular **Dundee Jazz Festival** (ⓦ www.jazzdundee.co.uk). In St Andrews, the **StAnza Poetry Festival** and the **On the Rocks Festival** (ⓦ www.ontherocksfestival.com) are annual highlights. As with all Scottish cities, Hogmanay (New Year's Eve) is a big event, with fireworks lighting up the skies at midnight. Only the bravest, however, would attempt **Dundee's New Year's Day** tradition of the **'Ne'er Day Dook'** when hardy types plunge into the River Tay at Broughty Ferry. The chilly water is reputed to cure even the worst of Hogmanay hangovers!

🔺 *Scotland's sunniest city*

History

The site on which Dundee stands has been inhabited for
thousands of years. There are scant remnants of an Iron Age
settlement atop Dundee Law, and in the surrounding
countryside a number of even earlier Neolithic settlements
suggest thriving ancient communities. During the Middle
Ages, it became a prosperous mercantile city, trading with the
cities of the Hanseatic League in Germany, Scandinavia and the
Baltic Sea. Very little remains from those days: the city was
sacked by the English during their invasion of Scotland in the
mid-16th century, and was levelled again a century later by
Parliamentarian forces under Oliver Cromwell's lieutenant,
George Monk. Prosperity gradually returned during the 18th
century, but Dundee's boom years really began with the
Industrial Revolution. Its textile mills produced the canvas
sailcloth for the Royal Navy – and for the whaling ships that
sailed from Dundee to the Arctic Ocean. In return, the whale oil
that they brought back made it possible for Dundee's mills to
move from cotton- and linen-weaving to jute, the fibre that
made the city wealthy. By the mid-19th century, Dundee was a
single-industry town, with most of its workforce employed in
the jute mills. It also forged strong links with Calcutta and
surrounding Bengal, from where the raw jute was imported.

An overwhelmingly working-class city, Dundee's 19th- and
20th-century politics tended to be left of centre. Winston
Churchill, elected as the Liberal MP for the city in 1908, was
ousted in 1922 by the local Prohibitionist candidate Edward
Scrimgeour, who campaigned unsuccessfully to ban alcohol.

Other political mavericks who have represented Dundee constituencies include Gordon Wilson, one of the first Scottish National Party MPs, who represented Dundee East from 1974 to 1987, and the Labour MP Ernie Ross, who was responsible in 1981 for Dundee's twinning with Nablus in a gesture of solidarity with Palestinian resistance to Israeli occupation.

The textile industry declined during the second half of the 20th century, leading to high unemployment, but Dundee has successfully attracted a number of new industries, including biotechnology and pharmaceuticals, IT and software development, and computer gaming.

● *Cox's Stack was part of the world's largest jute factory*

Culture

Dundee has a thriving cultural scene, with its own repertory theatre (the only one in Scotland) that includes the **Scottish Dance Theatre**, and a highly acclaimed contemporary arts centre (see page 62). Two universities and a well-regarded art college also give Dundee a vibrant edge.

Among the natives of Dundee who have made their name on the world cultural stage are the actor Brian Cox, the writer AL Kennedy, poet William McGonagall (often referred to as the 'world's worst poet' because of his disregard for metre or timing) and the lead singer of the pop band Deacon Blue, Ricky Ross. Dundee is probably best known, however, in a cultural sense as the home of Desperate Dan, Dennis the Menace and all the other characters in *The Beano* and *The Dandy*, the perennially popular comics produced by DC Thomson – indeed, there is even a statue of Dan himself in the centre of the city (see box page 52).

Japanese architect Kengo Kuma's adventurous design for a dazzling new museum, slated to become the centrepiece of a rejuvenated Dundee waterfront area, was selected in November 2010 from a shortlist of proposals presented by some of the world's leading architects. Kuma's design for **V&A Dundee**, to be built in association with London's Victoria and Albert Museum, will dominate the waterfront from its site at Craig Harbour and is expected to raise the city's tourism profile worldwide. It is due to open in 2014.

◗ *Broughty Beach*

MAKING THE MOST OF
Dundee

Shopping

Dundee's main shopping mall is the huge and stylish **Overgate Centre**, occupying an entire block in the centre of the city and providing plenty of space for numerous big brand and other shops, catering for most needs. Heading north from the High Street and City Square, **Murraygate** is lined with standard high street names, including a number of mobile phone and electrical retailers. Another shopping centre, the **Wellgate Centre**, can be found at the north end of Murraygate. It's a little less upmarket than the Overgate Centre, with stores offering great cut-price value. On Chapel Street, off the High Street, the **Forum Centre** has an eclectic mix of stores, mainly offering cut-price products and services, but shows its age.

A newer venture is the **City Quay** shopping centre on the north side of Victoria Dock (opposite Frigate *Unicorn*), boasting a range of factory outlet shops.

For everyday shopping, the largest supermarket close to the city centre is the big Tesco store on Riverside Drive, about five minutes' walk from the railway station, and there are numerous smaller shops close to the university area along Perth Road.

Dundee is a little short on quirky, independent shops with character. However, an honourable mention must go to **Dundee Contemporary Arts**, which has a shop that sells fine-art books, designer jewellery and ceramics, prints and all sorts of other really attractive gifts (see page 64). For a different shopping experience, visit **Dens Road Market**, north of the city centre. With its cavernous sheds packed with stalls selling genuine antiques, vintage clothing, bric-a-brac, second-hand furniture and kitchen equipment, it's a bargain-hunter's paradise, and offers the chance of really valuable finds.

⬥ *City Quay is the place to go for outlet shops*

Eating & drinking

Like most of Scotland, Dundee has enjoyed an eating and drinking revolution in recent years, and a city which once regarded the most basic Italian, Indian and Chinese establishments as the ultimate in exotic sophistication now revels in Thai, Mexican, Turkish, Asian-fusion, French and Spanish dining. That said, traditions linger. This is a student town, so fast food prevails, from pizzas and kebabs to some of the best fish and chips in the world.

Drinking has undergone changes, too. As well as old-fashioned pubs, every part of the city now has cafés, brasseries and wine bars serving wines from all over the world, cocktails and imported beers, as well as an ever-growing list of tasty ales from Scottish micro-breweries. It sometimes seems that there is a bar on every street corner (and another halfway down the block) and while many pubs have had a makeover in recent years, there are still plenty of classic old drinking spots graced by Victorian frosted glass, decorative bar mirrors and carved and panelled woodwork. All bars and restaurants are now smoke-free within, and some bars have outdoor spaces where smokers can enjoy their vice beneath patio heaters. Outside others, hardened addicts huddle in doorways for a quick nicotine fix.

Dundee is also famous for cakes, scones and pastries, and there are still a number of genteel old-fashioned tearooms serving great mid-morning snacks and more elaborate afternoon teas.

But if you're more into partying till the wee hours than sipping tea in the afternoon, you'll be pleased to discover

Dundee's thriving late-night culture. Major clubs stay open until at least 02.00 most nights, and often until 03.00 on Friday and Saturdays. Most bars open no later than midday (and some as early as 10.00) and stay open until at least midnight. Restaurant opening hours vary, with some brasserie-bars serving food all day, while more formal restaurants generally serve lunch 12.00–15.00 and dinner from around 19.00, with last orders at 21.00–22.00.

⬧ *The university district's Speedwell Bar has a listed interior*

Entertainment

For a smallish city, Dundee punches well above its weight in terms of entertainment, whether it's high art or low comedy, with venues ranging from cosy pubs to giant clubs. The city's biggest civic venue, the **Caird Hall**, has a long tradition of hosting leading national and international performances, while **Dundee Repertory Theatre** provides consistently entertaining and involving drama. Major ensembles, including Scottish Opera and Scottish Ballet, regularly visit the city. Several cinemas in or near the city centre serve up all the major mainstream releases, while the **Dundee Contemporary Arts** cinema also caters to arthouse tastes. Dundee's club scene is legendary, with a number of rival venues striving to provide the best DJs, foam parties and other themed nights. A large student body ensures that there is a steady demand for stand-up comedy and live music, hosted at venues throughout the city centre. Several annual festivals bring top-quality blues, jazz, rock and traditional music to the city, which also hosts a children's film festival and a mountain film festival each year.

Tickets for events at city-owned venues can be bought online, in person or by phone from the Dundee City Box Office ⓐ 6 City Square ⓣ 01382 434 940 ⓦ www.dundeecity.gov.uk ⓔ citybox@dundeecity.gov.uk

For what's on, see the classified section of the *Courier and Advertiser*, Dundee's daily newspaper, or the *Evening Telegraph*. Other useful sources are *The List* magazine ⓦ www.thelist.co.uk, published fortnightly, which mainly covers Edinburgh and Glasgow but also reviews and lists events and performances in

Dundee, and *The Skinny* Ⓦ www.theskinny.co.uk, a music, entertainment, food and drink paper aimed directly at Scotland's student population.

⬤ *The Repertory Theatre, or 'Rep'*

Sport & relaxation

The region's top two sports must be golf and football, with the world-class courses at Carnoustie and St Andrews – each less than 30 minutes from central Dundee – hosting the Open and other major events. Dundee is as football mad as the rest of the country, and during the season fans throng the city streets on Saturday afternoons in the bright orange strip of Dundee United. Walkers have some stunning scenery to enjoy in the glens of Angus and, if messing about in boats is your thing, there are the harbours of St Andrews and Broughty Ferry to enjoy.

Football
Dundee United is the city's major team, playing at their home stadium Tannadice Park. Dundee's other team is Dundee FC, with its home ground, Dens Park, literally moments away from United's.

Dundee United ⓐ Tannadice Park, Tannadice Street ① 01382 833 166 ⓦ www.dundeeunitedfc.co.uk
ⓔ boxoffice@dundeeunitedfc.co.uk ⓒ Contact club for fixtures
ⓝ Bus: 1A, 18, 19, 21 ① Admission charge

Dundee Football Club ⓐ Dens Park Stadium, Sandeman Street
① 01382 889 966 ⓦ www.dundeefc.co.uk ⓒ Contact club for fixtures ⓝ Bus: 1A, 18, 19, 21 ① Admission charge

Golf
Jack Nicklaus, Seve Ballesteros, Tiger Woods – name a golfing great – they're all certain to have taken to the fairway at

St Andrews. There are seven courses making up St Andrews Links, from the famed Old Course to the more forgiving 18-hole Strathtyrum Course and the nine-hole Balgove Course, which is a great starting point for children.

St Andrews Links ⓐ Bruce Embankment ⓣ 01334 466 666 ⓦ www.standrews.org.uk ⓔ enquiries@standrews.org.uk ⓛ Times vary, call or visit the website to book a round of golf ⓝ Bus: 91 ⓘ Admission charge

Skating

Ice-skating has seen something of a resurgence in popularity in recent years and the **Dundee Ice Arena** offers all manner of fun with its excellent facilities. As well as recreational skating open to all, there are lessons in figure skating and curling, as well as spectator events such as ice hockey. ⓐ Camperdown Leisure Complex, Camperdown Park ⓣ 01382 889 369 ⓦ www.dundeeicearena.co.uk ⓔ info@dundeeicearena.co.uk ⓛ Public skating 10.00–12.00, 14.30–16.30 Mon–Sat, 14.30–16.30 Sun (disco) ⓝ Bus: 2 ⓘ Admission charge

Spas

The **Apex City Quay** hotel provides a variety of pampering treatments based on a range of ancient Asian techniques, including Indian head massage and deep tissue massage. There's also a gym, hot tubs and a pool. ⓐ 1 West Victoria Dock Road ⓣ 01382 309 309 ⓦ www.yuspa.apexhotels.co.uk ⓔ enquiries@yuspa.co.uk ⓛ 07.00–22.00 Mon–Fri, 08.00–22.00 Sat & Sun ⓘ Admission charge

Accommodation

Dundee has a wide range of places to stay, from budget hostels and traditional bed-and-breakfast accommodation to three- and four-star hotels. Accommodation is located throughout the city, with numerous simple guesthouses and small hotels west of the centre in the Perth Road area, and also in the Broughty Ferry and Monifieth areas. Several of the major UK 'no-frills' hotel groups – including Travelodge, Premier Inns and Holiday Inn Express – have city-centre hotels, and these (although lacking in character) often offer excellent value especially at weekends. Most hotels and guesthouses can be booked online, and while it is usually possible to find somewhere to stay on arrival, making a reservation in advance is always advisable. Dundee plays host to a number of major academic and business conferences each year, and also accommodates large numbers of spectators attending major golf championships at Carnoustie and St Andrews. When such events are taking place, rooms can be harder to find.

The ambitious project to rejuvenate Dundee's waterfront (between the railway station and Victoria Dock) is likely to endow the city with several more new upmarket hotels over the next few years.

Dundee Backpackers Hostel £ This hostel – within an outstanding historic building – offers the best-value budget accommodation in the city, with a central location, choice of dorm beds, double and family rooms, laundry, self-catering facilities and Internet access. Weekly rates available.

ⓐ Gray's Close, 70–73 High Street ⓣ 01382 224 646
ⓦ www.hoppo.com ⓔ info@hoppo.com ⓝ All buses

Best Western Invercarse Hotel ££ This hotel on the western
outskirts of the city is mainly aimed at business travellers, but is
housed within a 19th-century mansion, and so has a bit of
character as well as the excellent facilities and well-appointed
modern rooms you'd expect, and (for anyone travelling by air) an
unbeatable location just three minutes away from the airport.
ⓐ 371 Perth Road ⓣ 01382 669 231 ⓦ www.bw-invercarsehotel.
co.uk ⓔ info@bw-invercarsehotel.co.uk ⓝ Bus: 6, 16B, 22, 22A,
39A, 73, 73A

Duntrune House ££ With four en-suite, bed-and-breakfast
rooms plus one self-catering apartment (weekly only), this
stylish 19th-century mansion stands in 3.25 hectares (8 acres) of
grounds in a peaceful location with marvellous views, but is only
minutes away from the city. Evening meals are available by
arrangement. ⓐ Duntrune, 8 km (5 miles) northeast of Dundee
ⓣ 01382 350 239 ⓦ www.duntrunehouse.co.uk ⓔ info@
duntrunehouse.co.uk ⓛ Mar–Oct

Fisherman's Tavern ££ A friendly, cosy inn with comfortable
modern en-suite rooms in converted cottages either side of the
original pub, which serves good grub and fine ales. Close
enough to the city centre to be a handy base, and quieter than
city centre hotels. ⓐ 10–16 Fort Street, Broughty Ferry
ⓣ 01382 775 941 ⓦ www.fishermanstavern.co.uk
ⓔ fishermans.broughtyferry@belhavenpubs.net ⓝ Bus: 5, 5A

Number Twenty-Five ££ Combining a restaurant, cocktail bar, nightclub and boutique hotel rooms – all within a stone's throw of the DCA, the Rep, and the city's top two clubs – this is very much a place for night owls rather than for those looking for a quiet night in, but it has added a dash of glamour to the city's accommodation scene. ⓐ 25 South Tay Street ⓣ 01382 200 399 ⓦ www.socialanimal.co.uk ⓔ numbertwentyfive@g1group.com ⓝ Bus: 22

Queen's Hotel ££ A Dundee landmark, the Queen's Hotel has been in business for more than a century, and is currently enjoying a new lease of life thanks to its location near to the DCA, the university and other lynchpins of Dundee's cultural quarter. Rooms are well-appointed, but on the small side; if possible go for a room with a view of the Firth, rather than one on the noisier Nethergate side of the building. ⓐ 160 Nethergate ⓣ 01382 322 515 ⓦ www.queenshotel-dundee.com ⓔ reception@queenshotel-dundee.com ⓝ Bus: 22

Apex City Quay Hotel £££ Unquestionably the smartest address in the city, this glamorous-looking, purpose-built property looks out over the Firth and the Victoria Dock, has a posh spa, health centre and pool and one of the city's better restaurants on-site. Within walking distance of the station and the city centre; five minutes from the airport. ⓐ West Victoria Dock Road ⓣ 01382 202 404 ⓦ www.apexhotels.co.uk ⓔ info@apexhotels.co.uk ⓝ Bus: 5B

Carnoustie Golf Hotel £££ This luxury hotel is the obvious choice for golfers, standing right next to Carnoustie's championship course. With 75 en-suite rooms (choose from sea or course views) it also has a large pool and an excellent spa. ⓐ The Links, Carnoustie ⓣ 08444 146 600 ⓦ www.oxfordhotelsandinns.com ⓔ reservations.carnoustie@ohiml.com

Hotel Broughty Ferry £££ Stunning new four-star designer-boutique hotel with just 16 luxury rooms but all the facilities you would expect from a bigger establishment, including a heated indoor pool, sauna and a good à la carte restaurant. ⓐ 16 West Queen Street, Broughty Ferry ⓣ 01382 480 027 ⓦ www.hotelbroughtyferry.co.uk ⓔ enquiries@hotel broughtyferry.co.uk ⓝ Bus: 5, 5B

The Landmark £££ This four-star hotel is a recent addition to the city's portfolio and adds a welcome whiff of luxury. A converted 19th-century faux-baronial mansion with modern additions, it stands in extensive landscaped grounds on the western edge of the city (but only 10 minutes from the centre and the airport). Facilities include a health centre and pool. ⓐ Kingsway West, Invergowrie ⓣ 01382 641 122 ⓦ www.thelandmarkdundee.co.uk ⓔ reservations@thelandmarkdundee.com ⓝ Bus: 5A, 5B

THE BEST OF DUNDEE

Dundee is a compact city and is easy to explore on foot. Good public transport makes outlying areas easy to reach, too. With a little forward planning, you can easily cram all its main attractions and activities into a long weekend or a short midweek break.

TOP 10 ATTRACTIONS

- **RRS *Discovery* and Discovery Point** The ship that took Captain Scott on his first Antarctic voyage offers a fascinating insight into early polar exploration (see pages 44–6).

- **Dundee Contemporary Arts** Explore interesting, even challenging exhibitions and installations at DCA; and don't forget to check out the café bar and shop (see page 62).

- **The McManus** Dundee's premier art gallery and museum, with some superb works of art from all over the world, stunningly presented. Allow several hours (see pages 53–4).

- **Dundee Law** Take the bus to the top of Dundee's own extinct volcano for a breathtaking panorama (see pages 57–9).

- **Broughty Ferry** Dundee's seaside suburb has an interesting museum housed in a dinky medieval castle, a couple of great pubs, a swan-filled harbour and a huge beach (see pages 68–76).

- **Verdant Works** This award-winning industrial heritage museum gives fascinating insight into the not-so-long ago world of the city that was once known as 'Juteopolis' (see pages 61–2).

- **St Andrews** For aficionados, a pilgrimage to the home of golf is mandatory. For others, there's a grim castle, a dramatic ruined cathedral, a long sandy beach and an aquarium replete with friendly seals (see pages 78–83).

- **Dundee Repertory Theatre** Consistently one of Britain's best companies for inventive drama and contemporary dance, with an excellent café-bar-restaurant (see page 63).

- **Frigate *Unicorn*** One of the oldest ships afloat, a visit below decks takes you back to the days of fighting sail (see page 46).

- **Take to the air** Take a light aircraft or helicopter flight from Dundee Riverside Airport to see the sights from above.

⏷ *The Discovery Point visitor centre*

Suggested itineraries

HALF-DAY: DUNDEE IN A HURRY

With just half a day to spare, it's best to restrict yourself to sights within the orbit of the city centre. A visit to the **RRS Discovery** is mandatory (allow about an hour to get through **Discovery Point**'s fascinating audiovisual displays). Then walk through the city centre to **The McManus**, taking a quick look at the medieval Old Steeple on the way. You should allow a couple of hours to browse The McManus's collection at an easy pace. Then stroll back through the centre to **Dundee Contemporary Arts** (DCA) and its excellent café-bar.

1 DAY: TIME TO SEE A LITTLE MORE

Spend the morning visiting Discovery Point and The McManus as above, then spend the afternoon at **Verdant Works**, the city's unique industrial heritage museum, before heading out to see what Dundee's many restaurants have to offer.

2–3 DAYS: SHORT CITY BREAK

With a few days to spare, you've time to spend a first day visiting Discovery Point and the nearby **Frigate** *Unicorn*, then visiting **Sensation** and taking in an exhibition at DCA. Spend the afternoon with a leisurely exploration of The McManus. On day two, treat yourself to a trip to the seaside – visit **Broughty Castle Museum**, walk along the esplanade for lunch at the **Glass Pavilion**, then, if you're a golfer, play a round at one of the **Monifieth** courses. On day three, take the bus to **St Andrews** for a day of sightseeing, followed by dinner at the **Peat Inn**.

LONGER: ENJOYING DUNDEE TO THE FULL

With more than three days at your disposal, you'll need a car to make the most of Dundee's attractive rural hinterland. Head north on the A928 to visit **Glamis Castle** and the **Angus Folk Museum** (about 30-minutes' drive from the city centre). Go on to Kirriemuir (about 20 minutes north of Glamis) to see the humble home where JM Barrie – the creator of Peter Pan – grew up, then drive up **Glen Clova** for dinner and a night at the cosy **Glen Clova Hotel**. Anglers should pack a rod for a morning's fishing next day, as the hotel has its own trout fishing nearby. Walkers can spend as long as they like exploring the lovely scenery of the glen, and in summer there are plenty of pleasant picnic spots.

▲ *Claypotts Castle, Broughty Ferry*

Something for nothing

Dundee offers plenty of things to do and see for free, ranging from exciting museums and art galleries to beaches, parks and gardens. Admission to the city's keynote art gallery and museum, **The McManus**, costs nothing, and if you have more time on your hands than money to spare you could easily spend a morning or even a full day among its collections. **Broughty Castle Museum** (see pages 73–4), in Broughty Ferry, is also free. The city has plenty of parks and gardens for which there is no admission charge. The **Botanic Garden** (see page 57) is free to students and university staff, while the **Barnhill Rock Garden** (see page 68), west of the city centre, is free to all. At **Dundee Contemporary Arts**, for the cost of a coffee, visitors can watch printmakers at work in the studio next to the Jute café-bar. A trip to the top of Dundee Law, with its amazing views, costs no more than the bus fare. Admission to the historic **Mills Observatory** (see pages 60–61) atop Balgay Hill is also free, as is a peek through its still-working Victorian telescope, and there is only a token charge for the Observatory's planetarium shows (Oct–Mar). And, of course, **Broughty Beach**, with its golden sand and great sea views is free too. In summer, you can even swim for nothing if you're hardy enough.

When it rains

Dundee claims to be the sunniest city in Scotland, but that doesn't mean that it doesn't rain. Fortunately, most of the city's key sights are indoors and so can be enjoyed as easily on a rainy day as on a sunny one – in fact, the only major attractions that are fully exposed to Scottish weather are the beaches, parks and golf courses. Make the most of a rainy day by spending it at **The McManus**, where there are enough extraordinary exhibits and works of art to occupy you for hours. For families with children, the **Sensation** science centre (see page 49) with its entertaining hands-on exhibits is another great spot to spend time when it rains. The most interesting parts of **RRS *Discovery*** are below decks, so the historic vessel is really an all-weather attraction; the **Discovery Point** centre next to it, with its regular audiovisual shows, will also use up a wet-weather hour or so, as will the **Verdant Works** industrial heritage museum. For all-weather shopping, the **Overgate Centre** has a wide choice of retail outlets as well as plenty of places to eat and drink. There are matinee movies at the **Dundee Contemporary Arts** cinema, and there are also matinee performances for children and adults at **Dundee Repertory Theatre**. The **Olympia Leisure Centre**, with its pools and flumes, is due to be demolished as part of the redevelopment of Dundee's waterfront, but should be replaced by a newer and better pool and sports centre at Allan Street, northeast of Victoria Dock, by 2013.

On arrival

ARRIVING

Few cities in Britain have a setting as impressive as Dundee's. To the north of the city lie the rolling Sidlaw hills, covered with woods, fields and heathery moorland and in winter often capped by snow. To the east is the North Sea, to the west the patchwork fields of the fertile Carse of Gowrie, while in front of the city stretches the broad tidal estuary of the Firth of Tay. After all this scenic grandeur, arriving in the city itself is a little anticlimactic – something that should be remedied by 2014, with the building of a stunning new V&A Museum and a regenerated waterfront area.

By rail

Arriving by rail from the south, the visitor's first sight of the city is from the southern end of the historic Tay Rail Bridge, which curves for around 3.2 km (2 miles) across the Firth from the Fife shore. Looking down on the east side of the bridge, the stumps of the High Girders, the section of the original bridge which collapsed one stormy night in 1879, can be seen at low tide. On the other side, seals can often be seen basking on sandbanks upriver from the bridge. Trains from London and Edinburgh (via stations in Fife), Glasgow (via Stirling and Perth) and Aberdeen (via the East Coast route) all arrive at Dundee Tay Bridge Station, on the waterfront. There is a taxi rank at the station, but the city centre is less than five minutes' walk away. There is at least one train per hour between Dundee and Edinburgh and Dundee and Glasgow during the day, and at least four services daily from London King's Cross. There are also overnight services from London. Journey time from Glasgow or Edinburgh is around 90 minutes; from London, about 6 hours 30 minutes. Rail operators include FirstScotrail from Glasgow, Edinburgh, London and east coast cities; East Coast; and Virgin Trains, which operates the longest rail journey in Britain from Dundee to Penzance, a distance of just over 700 miles (see page 90).

By road

The fastest route to Dundee by car from Glasgow or Edinburgh is the M80 (from Glasgow) or M9 (from Edinburgh), then the A9 dual carriageway from Perth. Edinburgh is about an hour away from Dundee by road, Glasgow about 90 minutes. The A9 continues north from the city along the east coast of Scotland to Aberdeen, about 90 minutes' drive away. Buses from all three cities, from London, and other points in Scotland and England, arrive at Seagate Bus Station, five minutes' walk east of the city centre. Main coach operators to Dundee include Stagecoach and Scottish City Link (see pages 90–91). Buses to St Andrews and other points in Fife also depart from this terminus, crossing the Tay Road Bridge. A major ring road, the Kingsway, loops around the north side of the city from Invergowrie to the east side of town. Riverside Drive, which connects with the Kingsway at Invergowrie, runs along the coast and past the airport to the station.

If arriving from Edinburgh by road via Fife, the Tay Road Bridge swoops across the river to deposit you right in the middle of Dundee's waterfront area, only a few minutes'

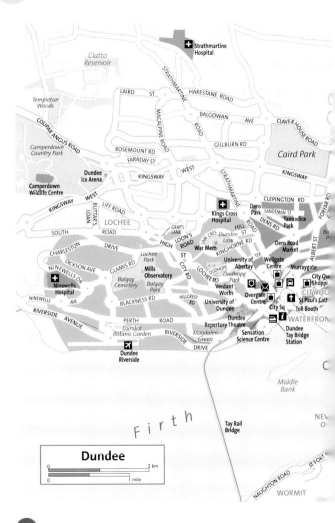

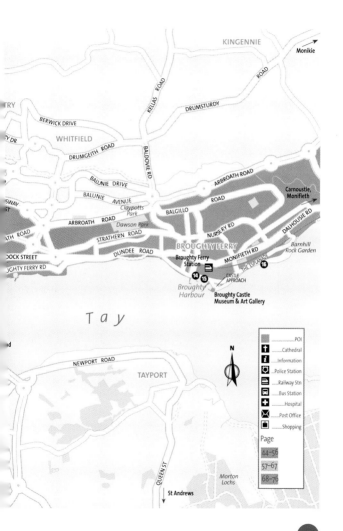

walk from the city centre. There is a large (pay) car park just north of the railway station, only a minute's walk from the Overgate, and more paid parking spaces beneath the bridge approaches and opposite the Olympia leisure centre. However, major redevelopment work on the waterfront, including the demolition of several major buildings and the redesigning of the bridge approaches, is likely to cause disruption to traffic in this part of town for some time and will reduce the amount of parking space available. There is also a large indoor car park at the west end of the Overgate shopping centre (off West Marketgait) and further car parking is available at the north end of South Tay Street, on the edge of the university campus area.

By air
Scot Airways (CityJet) flies to Dundee from London City Airport with a flight time of 75 minutes. Flybe flies from Belfast and Birmingham (see page 90). Dundee Riverside airport is less than 3.2 km (2 miles) from the city centre. Taxis meet all flights, and the 8X airport bus services operates 06.30–22.30 Mon–Sat with departures every 30 minutes and a five-minute journey time to the city centre. The airport has a café-bar and wireless Internet access.

A much wider choice of flights to London, other major UK cities and many mainland European cities is available from Edinburgh Airport, which is about an hour's drive from Dundee. Frustratingly, there is no direct public transport between Dundee and Edinburgh Airport; the fastest option is to take the Airlink 100 airport shuttle bus, which stops outside Edinburgh

Waverley Station (every 10 minutes, journey time 25 minutes) then a train to Dundee.

Several companies offer private taxi or minibus transfers between Edinburgh Airport and Dundee. These must be booked in advance (see page 91), but for more than two people travelling together they can be no more expensive than public transport, and for groups of four or more this is a cheaper option than taking the bus and train.

FINDING YOUR FEET

The Overgate and, at its east end, the City Square form the hub of the city, with the Nethergate and Perth Road extending westward from the Overgate, and the High Street and Murraygate extending east. Almost all of Dundee's main sights

● *The Sidlaw hills provide a dramatic backdrop to landings*

and attractions are within five- to ten-minutes' walk of the city centre. The University of Dundee campus, and Duncan of Jordanstone College of Art, are located between Nethergate/Perth Road and Hawkhill. Marketgait forms a busy inner ring road that loops around the city centre, with Dundee's other major educational establishment, the University of Abertay, located midway along its north side at Bell Street.

In terms of safety and security, Dundee has no problems that are not shared by other British cities, and the same common-sense rules apply – do not leave bags unattended, beware bag-snatchers and stay in well-lighted areas after dark. Ward Street, where the city's nightlife is concentrated, can be rowdy after dark, especially late at night on weekends. Do not leave valuables in plain sight in parked vehicles, even in covered car parks – theft from cars is not uncommon.

ORIENTATION

Getting your bearings in Dundee is remarkably easy. The city rises from the waterfront on the Firth of Tay in a long crescent, while Dundee Law with its prominent war monument makes a handy landmark north of the city centre. If lost, simply head downhill, which will quickly bring you back to recognisable territory.

The city's seaside suburbs, Broughty Ferry, Monifieth and Carnoustie, lie in a chain along the North Sea coast, northeast of the city centre. On the opposite shore of the Firth of Tay, the small towns of Newport and Wormit are technically part of Fife, but for all practical purposes they, too, are little more than dormitory suburbs of Dundee.

GETTING AROUND

Dundee has no metro or tram system, but a good network of bus services operated by Travel Dundee and Stagecoach connects all points within the city, as well as outlying suburbs such as Broughty Ferry, Monifieth, Carnoustie and Invergowrie. Few bus journeys within the city limits take more than 20 minutes. Buses also link the city with outlying towns, including St Andrews, Kirriemuir, Forfar and Arbroath.

The city centre is very compact (it takes less than 20 minutes to walk across it in any direction), so it makes sense to walk between most of the major sights and attractions. Most of the city is not pedestrianised, but the Murraygate, a major shopping street east of the High Street, is traffic-free and traffic is not usually heavy elsewhere in the city centre.

⬤ *The (road) Bridge on the River Tay, looking towards Dundee*

For longer journeys, buses depart to all parts of the city from stops on the Overgate and from Seagate Bus station.

There are taxi ranks at the railway station and on the Overgate, and taxis can be used to travel to any part of the city or further afield. Taxis are metered; tips are welcomed but are not essential.

Bike hire

Rent bikes (and helmets) by the hour, half-hour, day or week from **Spokes Cycles** (ⓐ 272 Perth Road ⓣ 01382 666 644 ⓦ www.spokescycles.net) in Dundee and St Andrews.

Car hire

Car hire is a luxury, not a necessity in Dundee, unless you plan to spend a lot of time exploring its rural hinterland. A combination of foot, bus and taxi will take you pretty much anywhere you want to go (even into the Angus Glens). However, for more than two people travelling together, car hire can be an affordable and more flexible alternative to public transport, especially for those planning to make several excursions outside the city centre. Alamo, Avis, Arnold Clark, Europcar and Hertz all have rental locations in or near the city centre and will deliver vehicles for pick-up at Dundee Riverside Airport (see page 90).

▶ *Caird Hall at the south end of City Square*

THE CITY OF
Dundee

Introduction to city areas

Since the Middle Ages, Dundee has grown east and west, spreading along the north shore of the Firth of Tay in a long crescent. In recent decades, the city has absorbed the formerly separate communities of **Broughty Ferry** and Monifieth, northwest of the centre, and Invergowrie, to the east. Dundee Law, a 174-m (571-ft) hill, overlooks **the city centre**. The Nethergate, Overgate, Murraygate and Wellgate are the city's main shopping streets, forming a continuous strip running parallel to the waterfront and a couple of blocks inland. West of the centre, the University of Dundee campus, Duncan of Jordanstone College of Art and associated buildings have merged to create a lively **university quarter** between the Nethergate and Hawkhill. Dundee has existed as a town for almost 1,000 years, but it is very much a modern city. Most of the city centre dates from the 19th century, when Dundee was an industrial boomtown. With the collapse of its heavy industries in the 1960s, many mill and factory buildings were demolished and the city's docks were filled in to create the approaches to the new Tay Road Bridge. The face of the city continues to change. The entire waterfront area, between the city centre and the river, is undergoing an ambitious urban renewal programme of demolition and rebuilding, which is unlikely to be complete until 2014.

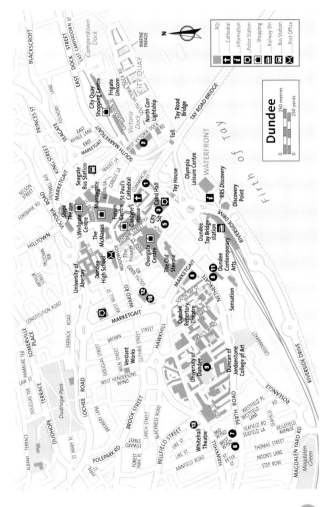

The city centre

Dundee's city centre is a compact area, and is most easily negotiated on foot, with the large, modern Overgate shopping centre as its main hub. Its most prominent landmark is the square steeple of St Mary's, Dundee's parish church and one of the city's few surviving medieval buildings. Another main shopping street, Reform Street, leads north from the Overgate, with the pompous, pillared portico of Dundee High School at its north end. More shops can be found along Murraygate, which leads east from the High Street and the city centre. The waterfront and the railway station are just two blocks south of the city centre, less than five minutes' walk away.

SIGHTS & ATTRACTIONS

Discovery Point & RRS *Discovery*

The Royal Research Ship *Discovery* is Dundee's signature landmark, now permanently moored in the former ferry dock on the waterfront, opposite Tay Bridge railway station. The three-masted vessel was commissioned by Sir Clement Markham, president of the Royal Geographical Society, for the RGS's 1901 expedition to the Antarctic, led by Captain Robert Falcon Scott. Returning from the Antarctic in 1904, *Discovery* was bought by the Hudson's Bay Company and served as a cargo vessel for more than 20 years, before returning to Antarctica for two more scientific expeditions in 1925 and 1929. She later became a training vessel, and until 1979 was moored on the Thames in central London, where she gradually became near-derelict.

Discovery was brought back to Dundee in 1986 and, after a painstaking restoration programme, became the hub of the Discovery Point visitor centre. Below decks are carefully designed cabins, storage and work areas – not a cubic inch of space is wasted. Next to the ship, the attractive former Tay ferry terminal, with its graceful glass-domed roof, now houses an excellent exhibition that reveals Dundee's central role in the opening up of the Arctic and Antarctic seas, which were explored by Dundee whaling captains long before explorers like Scott, Ernest Shackleton and the Norwegian Roald Amundsen

◆ RRS Discovery *at Discovery Quay*

arrived in search of glory. ⓐ Discovery Point, Discovery Quay
ⓣ 01382 309 060 ⓦ www.rrsdiscovery.com ⓔ admin@dundee
heritage.co.uk ⓛ 10.00–18.00 Mon–Sat, 11.00–18.00 Sun
(Apr–Oct); 10.00–17.00 Mon–Sat, 11.00–18.00 Sun (Nov–Mar)
ⓝ Bus: 5B ⓘ Admission charge

Frigate *Unicorn* & the *North Carr* lightship

Anchored in Victoria Dock, *Unicorn* is the biggest surviving
British-built wooden warship, and one of the oldest ships still
afloat. Launched in 1824, the 46-gun frigate never saw action,
and indeed never even set sail. Instead, she remained part of the
Royal Navy's reserve fleet until wooden warships became
obsolete. She was then used as a powder store and in 1873 was
towed to Dundee, where she served as a naval training and
headquarters ship until after World War II. Her impressive
cannon are still in place, and there are four cavernous decks to
explore, as well as the comfortably appointed captain's quarters.
Appropriately enough, her figurehead is a charging white
unicorn – which is also one of the national symbols of Scotland.
Also moored in Victoria Dock is another historic but slightly
more modern vessel, the red-painted *North Carr* lightship, which
was anchored near the mouth of the Tay to warn shipping away
from the North Carr Reef from 1933 until 1975, when she was
replaced by an automatic beacon. The *North Carr* lightship was
the last manned lightship in Scotland.
ⓐ South Victoria Dock Road ⓣ 01382 200 900 / 01382 542 516
ⓦ www.frigateunicorn.org/www.northcarrlightship.org
ⓛ 10.00–17.00 daily (Apr–Oct); 12.00–16.00 Wed–Fri, 10.00–
16.00 Sat & Sun (Nov–Mar) ⓝ Bus: 5B ⓘ Admission charge

Gardyne's House

Hidden away up a narrow close (alley) off the High Street, Gardyne's House is the oldest surviving building in central Dundee, with the exception of St Mary's Church. The five-storey, L-shaped complex, with its rough stonework and tall arched entryway, dates from around 1600, but the interior was rebuilt in the early 19th century and has since been thoroughly modernised during its conversion into a budget hostel, although many of its original medieval features remain in place. ❷ Gray's Close, 70–73 High Street ❶ 01382 224 646 ❿ www.hoppo.com ❶ Closed to non-residents ❶ Accommodation charge

The Howff

This medieval churchyard belonged to the Greyfriars (or Franciscans) whose monastery was destroyed during the Reformation. In 1564 it became the city's main cemetery, and its paths are lined with ancient weathered tombstones, some of them bearing skulls and other carvings and some eccentric epitaphs. During the Middle Ages it was used also as an open-air meeting place by Dundee's trade guilds, which gave it the name that is still in use today: *howff* is old Scots for 'gathering place'. ❷ Meadowside ❶ 01382 433 558 ❿ www.dundeecity. gov.uk ❶ 09.00–dusk daily

The Old Steeple (Dundee Parish Church)

Dundee's landmark city centre church is one of the city's few relics of its medieval past. It is, in fact, two churches in one, originally St Mary's and St Clement's. The square Gothic tower of St Mary's is one of the finest examples of Scottish medieval religious architecture, and was completed around 1460, about 20 years after construction of the main church building began. Its size and grandeur are evidence of Dundee's prosperity during the Middle Ages, although its present quite immaculate appearance is the result of an extensive restoration in the late 19th century by one of Britain's leading architects of the Victorian era, Sir George Gilbert Scott, who also designed Dundee's McManus Galleries and London's St Pancras station and Albert Memorial. The interior (like that of most Scottish churches) is surprisingly plain. The original was burned out in 1547 when Dundee was sacked during Henry VIII's notorious

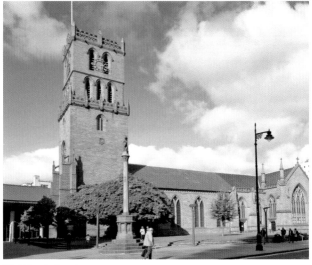

● *St Mary's Church*

'Rough Wooing' of Scotland; after the English left, the ascendancy of the ascetic-minded Protestant faith ensured that there would be no restoration of its former ornate grandeur. In the former kirkyard stands Dundee's original Mercat (Market) Cross, which once marked the heart of the city's commercial life. The carved stone pillar, erected in 1586, is topped by a modern replica of its original unicorn sculpture – the symbol of Scotland that once crowned such market crosses in all Scottish towns and cities. ❷ Nethergate ❶ 01382 226 271 ❿ www.dundee stmarys.co.uk ❷ office@dundeestmarys.co.uk ❹ 10.00–12.00 Tues, Thur & Fri (July & Aug); mass 11.00 Sun ❷ Bus: 22

Sensation (Dundee Science Centre)

The Dundee Science Centre is dedicated to proving that science can be fun, with dozens of hands-on exhibits that encourage children (and parents) to experiment. Tinker with robots, watch live science shows, learn about surgery and cybernetics or join a dig for dinosaur fossils. Sensation claims to be the only British science centre that challenges all five senses, hence its brand name. It also has an acceptable café, serving snacks, drinks and light meals. ❷ Greenmarket ❶ 01382 228 800 ❿ www.sensation.org.uk ❹ 10.00–17.00 daily; last admission 1 hour before closing ❷ Bus: 5B ❶ Admission charge

Tay Road Bridge

The 2.25-km (1½-mile) Tay Road Bridge was acclaimed as an engineering triumph when it opened in 1966, giving Dundee, for the first time, a fixed road link across the Firth of Tay to Fife and points south. It replaced a shuttle ferry service that had

previously operated between Newport in Fife and the ferry terminal that has since been turned into Discovery Point. It is still one of the longer road bridges in Europe, and in good weather there are great views from its pedestrian walkway eastward to the mouth of the Firth, the North Sea, Broughty Ferry and its castle, and the sandy Barry Buddon promontory.
ⓐ Marine Parade ❶ 01382 221 881 ⓦ www.tayroadbridge.co.uk
Ⓝ Bus: 5B

CULTURE

Caird Hall & City Square

Dundee's spacious city square is dominated by the lengthy façade of the Caird Hall, the city's grandest concert venue, which often hosts classical ensembles. In its day, it was the longest

⬥ *The McManus*

THE TAY RAIL BRIDGE DISASTER

When it first opened for traffic in 1878, the Tay Rail Bridge was described as 'one of the most gigantic works of mankind'. It was as much a triumph for its designer, Sir Thomas Bouch, as it was for the North British Railway Company, which was in a race with its great rival, the Caledonian Railway Company, to open up rail routes to Scotland. This was the heyday of Victorian free-market capitalism. The bridge was built in a rush and on the cheap. As a result, when on 28 December 1879 an extraordinarily powerful North Sea gale hit a train crossing the lofty 'High Girders' section, it collapsed, taking 90 passengers to their deaths. A new bridge was completed in 1886. It cost twice as much as the first, and still carries trains across the Tay. The stumps of the columns that toppled in 1879 can still be seen at low tide. The locomotive which pulled the fatal train was salvaged and put back into service. With typically Dundonian dark humour, it was nicknamed 'The Diver' by local railwaymen.

concert hall in the world (John Lennon, opening a Beatles concert there in 1967, called out: 'Can you hear us at the back there in Perth?'). Other legendary acts to have played the Caird Hall include Dame Nellie Melba, Paul Robeson, Gracie Fields, and rock giants like Led Zeppelin, The Who, Jethro Tull and Emerson, Lake and Palmer. The Caird Hall was a gift to the city from one of its many jute millionaires, Sir James Caird. King George V laid its foundation stone in 1914, but work was not completed until 1923. Sir James, in Dundee's tradition of aiding polar exploration, also helped to finance Ernest Shackleton's Antarctic expedition in the *Endurance*. When Shackleton made his epic open-boat journey across the Antarctic Ocean to South Georgia in 1916, after the *Endurance* became trapped in the ice, he named his fragile 7-m (23-ft) whaleboat the *James Caird*, in honour of his patron, and he is still immortalised as a patron of Antarctic exploration by the James Caird Society. In summer, the square is

THE MAN BEHIND DESPERATE DAN

Across from the north side of the square stands a larger-than-life statue of a larger-than-life comic character, Desperate Dan – one of the stars of a huge cast of characters brought to life by the Dundee publishing firm DC Thomson & Co in comics including *The Dandy*, *The Beano*, *Topper*, *Wizard* and *Hotspur*.

Desperate Dan – so macho that he shaves with a blowtorch and eats pies containing an entire cow, horns and all – first appeared in *The Dandy* in 1937. He was the brainchild of Dudley D Watkins (1907–69), who joined DC Thomson straight from Glasgow School of Art in 1925 and who created some of the company's most enduring characters – not just Desperate Dan, whose strips Watkins drew until his death in 1969, but also Oor Wullie, The Broons, Lord Snooty and others that continue to be produced in the 21st century.

often a venue for small-scale funfair attractions, and at
Christmas time it usually features an open-air skating rink.
Ⓐ City Square ☎ 01382 434 451 ⓦ www.cairdhall.co.uk
ⓔ cairdhall@dundeecitygov.uk ⏱ Box office: 09.30–16.30
Mon–Fri, 09.30–13.30 Sat ⓘ Admission charge

The McManus

Housed in a splendid Victorian Gothic building (originally named
the Albert Institute, in memory of Prince Albert, Queen Victoria's
Prince Consort) that is typical of the architecture of 'Juteopolis' in
its 19th-century heyday, the McManus has undergone a full-scale
refurbishment programme that was completed in 2009. Since
reopening, it has flourished as a remarkable museum with
collections that highlight every aspect of the city's past, including
its surprisingly extensive web of historical connections with India,
Africa, and other far-flung parts of the former British Empire. The
fine-art collection is outstanding, with more than 4,000 prints,
watercolours, oil paintings and sculptures, including a particularly
strong portfolio of 19th- and 20th-century Scottish painters, many
of them from the collection gifted to the city by James Guthrie
Orchar. There is also a good decorative arts collection, among the
highlights of which is a collection of Scottish Provincial
silverware. The social history collection sheds light on Dundee's
rapid transformation in the 19th century into a major locus for
shipbuilding, industry and whaling.

In the gardens outside The McManus, a bronze plaque
commemorates the 16 Dundonians who volunteered for the
International Brigades and were killed fighting against fascism
during the Spanish Civil War – a reminder of the city's long

> **THE UNFORTUNATE TAY WHALE**
> One of the McManus's best-loved exhibits is the skeleton of the legendary 'Tay Whale'. In 1883, this unfortunate 41-foot humpback whale turned up in the Firth of Tay, presumably unaware that it was entering the home waters of one of the world's biggest whaling fleets. It was prompted harpooned. The whale escaped after a long chase, but died of its wounds. Its floating corpse was recovered a week later, and was bought by a Dundee whale-oil merchant. After the remains were rendered down for oil, the skeleton was put on display and sent on tour. After visiting most of Britain's major cities, it returned to Dundee and its bony remains and tragic tale have enthralled generations of Dundee children ever since.

history of left-wing resistance. ❷ Albert Square ❶ 01382 307 200 ⓦ www.themcmanus-dundee.gov.uk ⓔ themcmanus@dundeecity.gov.uk ⓛ 10.00–17.00 Mon–Sat, 12.30–16.30 Sun ⓝ Bus: 15, 17

RETAIL THERAPY

The vast Overgate shopping centre dominates the city centre, housing a branch of Debenham's and an array of other major high-street names. A handful of shops in the city centre show some individuality. Down on the waterfront, City Quay makes an effort to create a new retail hub beside Victoria Dock.

JA Braithwaite This gorgeous old tea and coffee shop seems hardly to have changed since it opened here in the mid-19th century. With coffee beans ground in-house and its tea blended to customers' specifications, the smell as you walk through the door is wonderful. It also sells its own blends. ⓐ 6 Castle Street ⓣ 01382 322 963 ⓛ 09.00–18.00 Mon–Sat

TAKING A BREAK

Bon Appetit ££ ❶ Fine French bistro-style food, made from fresh, locally sourced ingredients. The menu changes with the

⬥ *Inside Braithwaite's tea and coffee shop*

seasons and there is a good wine list. Not the best choice for those in a rush – everything is cooked to order with loving care. ⓐ Exchange Street ⓣ 01382 809 000 ⓦ www.bonappetit-dundee.com ⓔ info@bonappetit-dundee.com ⓛ 12.00–14.00, 17.30–21.30 Mon–Thur, 12.00–14.00, 18.00–22.30 Fri & Sat, closed Sun

Metro Bar and Brasserie ££ ❷ The restaurant of this shiny modern hotel overlooks the dock where the Frigate *Unicorn* is moored and serves a tasty and varied menu that ranges from brasserie staples to some interesting fusion choices. ⓐ Apex City Quay Hotel, West Victoria Dock Road ⓣ 01382 202 404 ⓦ www.apexhotels.co.uk ⓔ dundeemetrorestaurant@apexhotels.co.uk ⓛ 12.00–14.30, 18.00–21.30 daily ⓝ Bus: 5B

AFTER DARK

Dundee has never been short of bars and pubs – indeed, there seems to be a drinking establishment on virtually every street corner in the city centre. However, the city's acknowledged nightlife hotspot is South Ward Road, where two rival nightlife colossi compete for the attention of the city's ravers.

Caird Hall ❸ The city's grandest venue, located on the handsome pedestrianised City Square, hosts stand-up comedy, rock, pop, jazz and musicals as well as classical concerts, ballet and opera. ⓐ City Square ⓣ 01382 434 451 ⓦ www.cairdhall.co.uk ⓔ cairdhall@dundeecitygov.uk ⓛ Box office: 09.30–16.30 Mon–Fri, 09.30–13.30 Sat

The university quarter

Dundee's university quarter occupies several blocks between the Nethergate – and its western extension, Perth Road – in the south and Hawkhill to the north, with Duncan of Jordanstone College of Art sitting at the junction of Nethergate and Perth Road. Around the campus buildings there are plenty of lively pubs, bars and cafés and shops catering to student needs.

🚍 Bus: 2, 5A, 6, 11, 12

SIGHTS & ATTRACTIONS

Dundee Botanic Garden

The University of Dundee's spacious botanic garden occupies a south-facing slope that looks out over the Tay. Committed to education, research and conservation, it features large outdoor gardens where native species from all over Britain are tended, as well as glasshouses that shelter exotic species from the tropics, the Mediterranean and the world's deserts. With its streams and pools, the garden is a pretty place for a stroll at any time of year, and it also has a daytime café and a plant and gift shop. ❸ Riverside Drive ☎ 01382 381 190 🌐 www.dundee.ac.uk/botanic ✉ botanicgardens@dundee.ac.uk 🕐 10.00–16.30 daily (Mar–Oct); 10.00–15.30 daily (Nov–Feb) 🚍 Bus: 5B ❶ Admission charge

Dundee Law

The Law is Dundee's principal natural landmark. An extinct volcanic plug, it looms above the city to a height of 174 m (571 ft)

and is believed to have been the site of the earliest Iron Age settlement in the area. It is often referred to as the Law Hill, which is a tautology – *law* means 'hill' in Scots. It's well worth making the trip to the top (preferably by bus, as the hill is surrounded by dull residential suburban streets) just for the amazing views. On a clear day, the Cairngorms can be seen beyond the Sidlaw hills to the north, while the silvery Firth of Tay sweeps eastward to the North Sea and narrows as it stretches westward towards Perth.

◭ *Magdalen Green and its bandstand*

The hill is crowned by the Law Monument, which commemorates the local soldiers who were killed during World War I and World War II, and atop which a beacon is lit four times a year, on the anniversary of the World War I Battle of Loos (25 Sept); United Nations Day (24 Oct); Armistice Day (11 Nov); and Remembrance Sunday. There are scanty remains of an Iron Age fort, which was the earliest human settlement in the Dundee area. ⓐ Law Road ⓝ Bus: 1S, 17, 28, 29, 51, 57, 59

Magdalen Green

This crescent of grassy lawns, just a short walk downhill from the University of Dundee's main campus area, looks out over the River Tay and the grand arc of the Tay Rail Bridge towards Wormit (at the Fife end of the bridge) and the green hills of Fife. At low tide, seals can often be seen basking on the sandbanks just west of the arches of the railway bridge. Until the early 19th century, the tideline of the Firth of Tay reached as far as the modern railway line, which now forms the southern perimeter of the Green. Everything seaward of the railway is the result of ambitious land reclamation works, which began with the landscaping of Magdalen Green from a formerly barren stretch of rocky foreshore in the early 1840s, inspired by Dundee's Provost, Alexander Lawson.

The Green's most-loved landmark, the prettily painted old cast-iron bandstand that occupies pride of place in the centre of this green space, was placed here in 1889. Saved from the scrapyard after being allowed to rust for many years, it was restored in 1991, but further work is needed to keep it pristine. ⓐ Magdalen Yard Road ⓝ Bus: 5B, X42

THE WORLD'S WORST POET

It is almost impossible to pastiche the works of William Topaz McGonagall. Perhaps the most famous bad poet ever, McGonagall (1825–1902) was born in Edinburgh of poverty-stricken Irish parents who moved to Dundee in search of work. As a child, he worked in the handloom mills that were made redundant by the Industrial Revolution, then in Dundee's giant weaving factories. In his time off, he devoured the works of Shakespeare, before setting out to make a name for himself as a bard. Despite a total and painfully evident lack of poetic talent, McGonagall became a cult hero, filling music halls in Scotland, England and the United States with audiences who came to hear him declaim his *Poetic Gems* while in full Highland dress. These days, he'd be pulling in huge ratings on *The X Factor*.

Mills Observatory

Unique in Britain, the Mills Observatory is a full-time public astronomical viewing facility, standing near the summit of Balgay Hill, northwest of the University of Dundee campus. It was built in 1935 with funds bequeathed by yet another of Dundee's textile-industry philanthropists, John Mills, who was a keen amateur astronomer. Its 19th-century refracting telescope and the mini-planetarium beneath its 7-m (23-ft) dome – which, amazingly enough, is made of papier-mâché – are not exactly state-of-the-art, but they still work and afford visitors a star-viewing experience that is in many ways more fascinating than any digitally rendered computer display. ⓐ Glamis Road, Balgay Park ⓣ 01382 435 967 ⓦ www.dundeecity.gov.uk/mills ⓔ mills.observatory@dundeecity.gov.uk ⓛ 11.00–17.00 Tues–Fri, 12.30–16.00 Sat & Sun (Apr–Sept); 16.00–22.00 Mon–Fri, 12.30–16.00 Sat & Sun (Oct–Mar). Planetarium shows Oct–Mar only: check website for times ⓝ Bus: 6, 16B, 22, 22A, 39A, 73, 73A

Verdant Works

Until the 1960s, Dundee's skyline was dominated by dozens of 'stacks', the tall chimneys of the city's coal-powered jute-weaving mills. The city's fortunes in the 19th century were built on cotton and jute weaving, but after World War II the textile industry declined and almost all the mills closed. Verdant Works is the sole survivor, and is now an award-winning visitor centre that brings the everyday life of the mills and their mainly female

🔺 Bringing the history of jute production to life at Verdant Works

workforce to life, with working machinery, offices and workshops preserved just as they were when the mill was in operation, and audio recordings of reminiscences of life in the mill from its retired workers. ⓐ West Henderson's Wynd ⓣ 01382 309 060 ⓦ www.rrsdisovery.com ⓔ admin@dundeeheritage.co.uk ⓛ 10.00–18.00 Mon–Sat, 11.00–18.00 Sun (Apr–Oct); 10.30–16.30 Wed–Sat (Nov–Mar); last admission 1 hour before closing ⓝ Bus: 28, 29 ⓘ Admission charge

CULTURE

Dundee Contemporary Arts

Since it opened in the 1990s, DCA has been a key player in rejuvenating the city, enlivening its arts and entertainment scene, placing Dundee on the map as a cutting-edge centre of creativity. Up to 70 artists work in DCA's studios (and some of them can be watched at work from the tables of the Jute Café Bar, which overlooks the DCA printmakers' studio). With an excellent brasserie-bar, a cinema that shows arthouse films as well as mainstream movies, DCA has become a lively hub of the city's creative life. ⓐ 152 Nethergate ⓣ 01382 909 900 ⓦ www.dca.org.uk ⓔ dca@dca.org.uk ⓛ Galleries: 10.30–17.30 Tues–Sat (until 20.30 Thur), 12.00–17.30 Sun. Print Studio: 11.00–21.00 Tues–Thur, 11.00–18.00 Fri & Sat ⓝ Bus: 22 ⓘ Admission charge

Dundee Repertory Theatre

Like the DCA (which is less than a minute's walk away), 'The Rep' has played a big part in putting the city on the cultural map. The

Rep's story is a rags-to-riches tale: founded in 1939, its original home was in a converted jute mill in Lochee. In 1982, it moved to its new home in this outstanding purpose-built venue that now houses both the Dundee Repertory Ensemble and Scottish Dance Theatre. Both groups tour worldwide, with the Dundee Repertory Ensemble taking works created here to venues as far away as Iran, Mexico and Japan. The Rep's creation *Sunshine on Leith*, a musical based on the works of The Proclaimers, proved to be an unlikely smash hit, and is still touring. ⓐ Tay Square ⓘ 01382 227 684 ⓦ www.dundeereptheatre.co.uk ⓔ info@dundeereptheatre.co.uk ⓒ Box office: 10.00–19.00 Mon–Sat (until 18.00 when no performance) ⓝ Bus: 22

🔺 *The Botanic Gardens*

RETAIL THERAPY

Most of Dundee's main retail outlets are east of the university quarter, in the city centre, but there are plenty of shops in this area that offer a different side of Dundee.

Dundee Contemporary Arts The DCA shop sells some beautiful ceramics, jewellery and textiles created by local artisans, prints from the on-site printmakers, gorgeous coffee-table art books, designer jewellery and entertaining and educational stuff for kids. ⓐ 152 Nethergate ⓣ 01382 909 900 ⓦ www.dca.org.uk/shop ⓔ dca@dca.org.uk ⓛ 09.30–18.00 Mon–Sat ⓝ Bus: 22

Groucho's Nick Hornby fans love this long-established rock emporium, which buys and sells new and used CDs, vintage vinyl and tapes, and sells other rock and roll essentials including tickets for most rock and pop events in Scotland and further afield. ⓐ 132 Nethergate ⓣ 01382 228 496 ⓦ www.grouchos. co.uk ⓔ info@grouchos.co.uk ⓛ 09.00–17.30 Mon–Sat, 12.00–16.30 Sun ⓝ Bus: 22

Sutherlands The Tartan Shop Every Scottish city has to have a tartan shop, selling kilts and accessories, gifts, souvenirs, cards and stationery. Sutherlands fills this slot on Dundee's Nethergate. ⓐ 90 Nethergate ⓣ 01382 224 709 ⓔ tartanshop@ hotmail.com ⓛ 09.00–17.30 Mon–Sat, 12.00–16.00 Sun ⓝ Bus: 22

TAKING A BREAK

The Deep Sea £ ❹ The best fish and chips in Dundee, arguably the best in Scotland, and possibly the best in the world. Eat in or take away. ➌ 81 Nethergate ➊ 01382 224 449 ➋ 09.30–18.30 Mon–Sat, closed Sun ➍ Bus: 22

Fisher and Donaldson £ ❺ The quintessential Scottish tearoom and bakery, this fourth-generation-run establishment offers superb cakes, breads, biscuits, scones, pastries and sandwiches. ➌ Whitehall Street ➊ 01382 223 488 ➐ www.fisher anddonaldson.com ➎ sales@fisheranddonaldson.com ➋ 08.00–16.45 Mon–Sat ➍ Bus: 22

⬥ *Jute Café Bar at DCA*

Agacan ££ Quirky and colourful, walls adorned with paintings by generations of budding artists from the nearby art college (some of whom are now quite famous), this small, friendly restaurant serves superb Turkish food. ⓐ 113 Perth Road ⓣ 01382 644 227 ⓛ 17.00–22.00 Tues–Sun ⓝ Bus: 5A, 5B

Dil'se ££ ❼ This excellent, modern Indian/Bangladeshi restaurant serves up a fine array of mouthwatering spicy dishes and a lavish, great-value Sunday afternoon buffet. ⓐ 99–101 Perth Road ⓣ 01382 221 501 ⓦ www.dilse-restaurant.co.uk ⓔ info@dilserestaurant.co.uk ⓛ 12.00–23.30 Mon–Thur, 12.00–24.00 Fri & Sat, 13.00–23.00 Sun (buffet 13.00–18.00) ⓝ Bus: 5A, 5B

Jute at Dundee Contemporary Arts ££ ❽ This popular brasserie-style café-bar-restaurant is well known for its imaginative and varied menu, with better than average options for children. ⓐ 152 Nethergate ⓣ 01382 909 246 ⓦ www.dca.org.uk ⓔ dca@dca.org.uk ⓛ 10.30–21.30 daily ⓝ Bus: 22

AFTER DARK

Dundee University Students Union ❾ The throbbing heart of on-campus nightlife, with something happening every night of the week, including karaoke nights, DJs and occasional live music and comedy acts. ⓐ Airlie Place ⓣ 01382 386 060 ⓦ www.dusa.co.uk ⓔ info@dusa.co.uk ⓛ 10.00–24.00 Sun–Mon, 10.00–02.30 Tues–Sat ⓝ Bus: 22 ⓘ Open to students only

Fat Sam's ⑩ Dundee's top nightlife hub opened in 1983 and has gone from strength to strength as a fabulous dance club and live music venue. Its foam parties are legendary, and it hosts the city's biggest Hallowe'en and Hogmanay parties. ⓐ 31 South Ward Road ⓣ 01382 228 181 ⓦ www.fatsams.co.uk ⓔ colin@fatsams.co.uk ⓛ Hours vary depending on event: check website for details ⓝ Bus: 51; club's own minibus pickup and drop-off service available

IDCA Cinema ⑪ Dundee's best cinema shows a well-chosen mixture of mainstream movies, arthouse releases and children's films. ⓐ 152 Nethergate ⓣ 01382 909 900 ⓦ www.dca.org.uk ⓔ dca@dca.org.uk ⓛ Contact box office or see local listings ⓝ Bus: 22

Liquid ⑫ Fat Sam's upstart rival opened in 2008 and is just a few steps away. Liquid is really three venues in one, with the main Liquid and Envy rooms, plus VIP booths on the mezzanine floor. ⓐ 21 South Ward Road ⓣ 01382 205 551/0845 313 2584 ⓦ www.liquidclubs.com ⓔ dundee@liquidclubs.com ⓛ Hours vary: check website ⓝ Bus: 51

Whitehall Theatre ⑬ This venerable theatre hosts musicals, light opera, dance performances, tribute bands, vintage rock 'n' roll acts, stage hypnotists and stand-up comedy – in short, good old-fashioned fun. ⓐ 12 Bellfield Street ⓣ 0871 702 9486 ⓦ www.whitehalldundee.co.uk ⓛ Contact box office or see local listings

Broughty Ferry, Monifieth & Carnoustie

Broughty Ferry is Dundee's own seaside. At the mouth of the Firth of Tay, its 15th-century castle overlooks a former fishing harbour that grew up in the 18th and 19th centuries. Beyond the castle, the Tay opens into the North Sea and a long sweep of sandy beach and dunes extends all the way north to Monifieth. Both of these formerly independent communities are now residential suburbs of Dundee. A little further north, Carnoustie has its own long stretch of sands and dunes, and is known internationally for its fine golf courses, which are rated among the finest traditional links courses in the world.

SIGHTS & ATTRACTIONS

Barnhill Rock Garden

This attractive green space overlooking the dunes and sands along the foreshore was created in 1955 on the site of a former golf course and the abandoned Carmyllie stone quarry. Since then, it has been embellished and extended, with snowdrop woods, rock gardens, shrubberies, streams and tadpole ponds and picnic tables. ⓐ The Esplanade, Barnhill ⓣ 07985 878 515 ⓦ www.barnhillrockgarden.org.uk ⓝ Bus: 39A, 73A, 73B

Barry Mill

Porridge lovers should visit this historic watermill on Sundays, when its traditional millstones are put into use to grind grain

⬧ *Visit Barry Mill to see oatmeal being ground*

from a local farm into the most authentic oatmeal in Scotland. The mill, with its 4.7-m (15-ft) overshot wheel, is one of only three working watermills left in Scotland, and watching its antiquated machinery in action is a fascinating experience. There are also some pleasant walks along its mill lade – the artificial channel that leads water from the Barry Burn to drive the mill wheel – and along the banks of the burn itself.
🅐 Barry, Carnoustie 🅣 0844 493 2140 🆆 www.nts.org.uk
🅔 barrymill@nts.org.uk 🅛 Mill: 12.00–17.00 Mon & Thur–Sat, 13.00–17.00 Sun (Apr–Oct) 🅝 Bus: 73, 73A 🅘 Admission charge

Broughty Beach

Broughty Beach is Dundee's seaside – a long sweep of gorgeous golden sand that stretches all the way from the mouth of the Tay to Monifieth and the Barry Buddon promontory. In summer, it can (weather permitting) be a great place for a picnic and a paddle, and it is also popular with windsurfers, beachcombers, kite-flyers and dog-walkers all year round. The beach joins seamlessly with Monifieth beach to the north, and extends all the way north to the Barry Buddon peninsula, which juts eastward into the North Sea. Parts of Barry Buddon are used as military firing ranges, but when live firing (indicated by red flags) is not taking place it is possible to walk along the coast all the way to Carnoustie. 🅐 Broughty Ferry Esplanade
🅝 Bus: 73, 73B

Broughty Harbour

Broughty Ferry's modestly pretty harbour once supported a herring-fishing fleet, but is now home to only a small flotilla of

sailing boats and a resident flock of swans. The community owes its name to the first ferry crossing that, in medieval times, linked Broughty to Tayport on the Fife shore. This made Broughty Ferry a place of considerable military importance, and in the late 15th century a castle was built to command the harbour. By the 19th century it had become derelict, but it still occupied a strategic spot, and so it was bought and modernised by the British Government to be used as a military outpost. As a result, sturdy stone ramparts, designed in the early 1860s, surround the original stone tower of the castle. The rest of Broughty Ferry is much less bellicose-looking, with a grid pattern of streets lined with distinctive two-storey houses and cottages spreading inland from the seashore. ⓐ Broughty Ferry
🚍 Bus: 5A, 5B

🔺 *Jet-skiing in Broughty Harbour*

Carnoustie Golf Club

Carnoustie Golf Club was founded in 1842, making it one of the ten oldest clubs in the world. Its par-72 championship course is rated among the world's toughest traditional links courses, and has hosted the Open Championship seven times, most recently in 2007. It hosted the Seniors' Open in 2010, and the Women's British Open in 2011. The championship course is complemented by the slightly less prestigious, but still demanding, Burnside Links and Buddon Links. ⓐ 20 Links Parade, Carnoustie ⓣ 01241 802 270 ⓦ www.carnoustie golfclub.com ⓔ golf@carnoustiegolfclub.com ⓛ Times vary: contact the club ⓝ Bus: 73, 73A ⓘ Charge for playing

⬥ Enjoy a round on the world-famous links at Carnoustie

Crombie Country Park

With 102 hectares (252 acres) of woodland and almost 8 km (5 miles) of forest paths laid out around Crombie Loch (a former reservoir), the country park provides a refuge for green woodpeckers, red squirrels, roe deer and flocks of waterfowl. ⓐ Monikie, off A92 ⓣ 01241 860 360 ⓦ www.angusahead.com ⓔ crombiepark@angus.gov.uk ⓛ Park: 09.00–21.00 daily (May–Aug); 09.00–dusk daily (Sept–Apr). Ranger Centre: 09.00–17.00 daily (Mar–Apr, Sept & Oct); 09.00–21.00 daily (May–Aug); 09.00–16.30 daily (Nov–Feb)

Monifieth Links

Four clubs – Broughty Golf Club, Ladies' Panmure, Grange and Monifieth – share this stretch of windswept bends and dunes on the North Sea shore, but Monifieth is the most prestigious, having hosted world-class contests including the 2007 Open. The Monifieth medal course is a demanding 6,094-m (6,665-yd) par 71, with heavy patches of rough, fast greens and constantly shifting winds that challenge even the professionals. ⓐ Princes Street, Monifieth ⓣ 01382 532 767 ⓦ www.monifiethgolf.co.uk ⓔ starter@monifiethgolf.co.uk ⓛ Times vary: contact the club ⓝ Bus: 73, 73A, 78, 79 ⓘ Charge for playing

CULTURE

Broughty Castle Museum & Art Gallery

Broughty Castle was built in 1496 and changed hands between English invaders and Scottish factions over the next century. It was built and owned by the aristocratic Masters of Gray, who owned lands and castles all over Tayside. It lay derelict from the mid-17th century until 1861, when it became a military fort and was extensively rebuilt. Decommissioned after World War II, it's now an interesting little museum with exhibits dedicated to Broughty's past as a fishing and whaling community, and an excellent art gallery that displays oil paintings and water colours from the huge collection gifted to Dundee by the 19th-century engineer and inventor James Guthrie Orchar.

ⓐ Castle Approach, Broughty Ferry ⓣ 01382 436 916
ⓦ www.dundeecity.gov.uk/broughtycastle ⓔ broughty@dundeecity.gov.uk ⓛ 10.00–16.00 Mon–Sat, 12.30–16.00 Sun (Apr–Sept); 10.00–16.00 Tues–Sat, 12.30–16.00 Sun (Oct–Mar)
ⓝ Bus: 5A, 5B ⓘ Admission charge

◯ *Dramatic skies over the Firth of Tay estuary*

RETAIL THERAPY

Broughty Ferry's charming town centre has a few attractive small arts and craft shops, including one rather good commercial art gallery.

Eduardo Alessandro Studios This colourful, creative commercial gallery and gift shop showcases paintings, prints, ceramics, and jewellery made by Scottish and other artists, designers and artisans. ⓐ 30 Gray Street ⓣ 01382 737 011 ⓦ www.east studios.com ⓔ mail@eaststudios.com ⓛ Mon–Sat 09.30–17.00, 12.00–16.00 Sun (July, Aug & Dec only) ⓝ Bus: 5, 5A

TAKING A BREAK

Fisherman's Tavern £ ⓮ Good pub grub, great choice of real ales and malt whiskies, authentic atmosphere and comfortable bedrooms for those who wish to stay overnight. ⓐ 10–16 Fort Street, Broughty Ferry ⓣ 01382 775 941 ⓦ www.fishermanstavern.co.uk ⓔ fishermans.broughtyferry@ belhavenpubs.net ⓛ 11.00–24.00 daily ⓝ Bus: 5, 5A

Visocchi's £ ⓯ A superb traditional ice-cream parlour and trattoria that has been a Broughty Ferry institution for generations. Excellent Italian home cooking. ⓐ 40 Gray Street, Broughty Ferry ⓣ 01382 779 297 ⓛ 10.00–16.00 Tues, 10.00–20.00 Wed, Thur & Sun, 10.00–22.00 Fri & Sat, closed Mon ⓝ Bus: 5, 5A

⬆ *The cosy Fisherman's Tavern*

The Glass Pavilion ££ ⑯ This shiny Art Deco building midway along the seafront has been a Broughty Ferry seaside landmark since the 1930s, and a recent makeover means it lives up to its name. Serves breakfast (the full Scottish), lunch, afternoon teas and an à la carte dinner. ⓐ The Esplanade, Broughty Ferry ⓣ 01382 732 738 ⓦ www.theglasspavilion.co.uk ⓔ info@theglasspavilion ⓛ 10.00–22.00 daily ⓝ Bus: 5, 5A

▶ *Glamis Castle*

OUT OF TOWN
trips

St Andrews

St Andrews is a charming small historic town that is home to Scotland's oldest university, and is even more famous as the birthplace of golf. Relics of its medieval heyday include the ruins of an impressive castle and an ancient abbey, and the huge East Sands beach. A small harbour is still home to a few fishing boats, but they are now outnumbered by sailing boats and motor cruisers.

St Andrews is compact; it takes no more than 15 minutes to walk from one end of town to the other, making sightseeing easy and public transport redundant. The gracious old quadrangles of the university are scattered around the town centre.

GETTING THERE

St Andrews is 21 km (13 miles) from Dundee. There are regular buses from Dundee Seafield Road bus station, taking approximately 30 minutes.

SIGHTS & ATTRACTIONS

British Golf Museum

Golf fanatics will find this museum, which opened in 1990, fascinating, and even long-suffering non-golfing partners may find a glimmer of interest in the multimedia displays that underline St Andrews' claim to be the unchallenged birthplace of the game. ⓐ Bruce Embankment ⓣ 01334 460 046 www.britishgolfmuseum.co.uk ⏱ 10.00–16.00 daily (Nov–Mar); 09.30–17.00 Mon–Sat, 10.00–17.00 Sun (Apr–Oct) Bus: 91 ⓘ Admission charge

Royal and Ancient Golf Club

A place of pilgrimage for golfers everywhere, the R&A is the seat of golf's most august club, the game's governing body and the Open Championship. ⓐ The Links ☎ 01334 460 000 www.randa.org.uk ⏱ Times vary: contact the club ⓝ Bus: 91 ⓘ Charge for playing

🔺 *The ruins of St Andrews Cathedral*

St Andrews Aquarium

This great family attraction features colourful denizens of coral reefs and tropical waters as well as no-less-fascinating creatures of the North Sea, from lobsters and seahorses to sharks and seals. ⓐ The Scores ⓣ 01334 474 786 ⓦ www.standrewsaquarium.co.uk ⓔ info@standrewsaquarium.co.uk ⓛ 10.00–17.00 daily (Feb–Dec); 10.00–17.00 Sat & Sun (Jan) ⓝ Bus: 91 ⓘ Admission charge

St Andrews Castle

Overlooking the sea, this dour stronghold was the seat of the powerful Archbishops of St Andrews until the religious wars of the 16th century, when it was besieged and finally part-destroyed. The 'bottle dungeon', carved out of the rock on which the castle stands, is its creepiest feature. ⓐ The Scores ⓣ 01334 477 196 ⓦ www.historic-scotland.gov.uk ⓛ 09.30–17.30 daily (Apr–Sept); 09.30–16.30 daily (Oct–Mar) ⓝ Bus: 91 ⓘ Admission charge

St Rule's Tower (St Andrews Cathedral)

St Rule's Tower is the only intact remnant of the once-grand St Andrews Cathedral, though parts of the cathedral's impressive cloisters can still be seen beside it. The view from the top of the ancient tower is breathtaking – as are the stairs that lead to it. ⓐ The Pends ⓣ 01334 472 563 ⓛ 09.30–17.30 daily (Apr–Sept), 09.30–16.30 daily (Oct–Mar) ⓝ Bus: 91 ⓘ Admission charge

Scotland's Secret Bunker

This huge man-made cavern, accessed through an innocent-looking farmhouse, was chosen to shelter the great and the good if World War III ever broke out. It's a chilling reminder of the Cold War mindset. ⓐ Troywood, 11 km (7 miles) south of St Andrews ⓣ 01333 310 301 ⓦ www.secretbunker.co.uk ⓔ mod@secretbunker.co.uk ⓛ 10.00–17.00 daily (mid-Mar–Oct) ⓘ Admission charge

CULTURE

The Barron Theatre

Part of the university, the Barron is home to eclectic and experimental theatre. It is normally open to non-students. ⓐ North Street ⓣ 01334 461 701 ⓦ www.standdrews.ac.uk ⓔ barron@standrews.ac.uk ⓛ Contact box office ⓘ Admission charge

● *St Andrew's undergraduates wear distinctive red gowns*

RETAIL THERAPY

St Andrews Links Golf Shops Four shops strategically located around the links, selling golf kit, presents and souvenirs. ⓐ Old Course, Links Clubhouse, 18th Green and Castle Course ① 01334 466 731 ⓦ www.standrews.org.uk ⓔ golfshops@ standrews.org.uk ① 08.00–18.00 daily ⓝ Bus: 91

TAKING A BREAK

The Vine Leaf ££ Great seafood, an excellent array of vegetarian choices and an imaginative wine list make this the best place to eat in central St Andrews. ⓐ 131 South Street ① 01334 477 497 ⓦ www.vineleafstandrews.co.uk ⓔ info@vineleaf standrews.co.uk ① 18.30–24.00 Tues–Sat, closed Sun & Mon

The Peat Inn £££ This award-winning restaurant is regarded as one of the best in Scotland, serving classic, French influenced dishes prepared using the freshest local produce. ⓐ Peat Inn, 10 km (6 miles) southwest of St Andrews ① 01334 840 206 ⓦ www.thepeatinn.co.uk ⓔ stay@thepeatinn.co.uk ① 12.00–13.30, 19.00–21.00 Tues–Sat, closed Sun & Mon

AFTER DARK

Most people head for the bright lights of nearby Dundee for a serious night out, but St Andrews has plenty of pubs; student nightlife focuses on the multiple venues of the Union.

The Inn at Lathones It's a bit out of town, but it is well worth the taxi ride to this award-winning music pub that hosts some top-level rock and folk performers. ⓐ Lathones, 11 km (6 miles) southwest of St Andrews ⓣ 01334 840 494 ⓦ www.innatlathones.com ⓔ lathones@innatlathones.com ⓛ See website for performance schedules ⓝ Bus: X26

St Andrews University Union The main Union venue (normally students only) hosts movie nights, live music and stand-up comedy. ⓐ North Street ⓣ 01334 461 701 ⓦ www.yourunion.net ⓔ barron@standrews.ac.uk ⓛ Main bar 12.00–02.00 Thur–Sat, 12.00–01.00 Sun–Wed ⓘ Admission charge for some events

ACCOMMODATION

McIntosh Hall £ Budget accommodation in a students' hall of residence in the town centre. ⓐ Abbotsford Crescent ⓣ 01334 467 035 ⓦ www.discoverstandrews.com ⓔ mchall@st-andrews.ac.uk ⓝ Bus: 91

Albany Hotel ££ Elegant but surprisingly affordable town-house hotel with 22 rooms, all en-suite, and a cosy lounge and bar. ⓐ 56–58 Shore Street ⓣ 01334 477 737 ⓦ www.thealbanystandrews.co.uk ⓔ info@thealbany standrews.co.uk ⓝ Bus: 91

The Inn at Lathlones ££ and **The Peat Inn £££** (see above and opposite, for contact details) both offer comfortable rooms outside the town centre.

Angus & its glens

North of Kirriemuir and the A926 highway the countryside
changes dramatically from tidy farmland to wilder hills and
moors. The three Angus glens – Isla, Prosen and Clova – plunge
deep into this spectacular terrain. For a short break, Clova is the
most accessible and attractive of the three.

GETTING THERE

It is easiest to explore Angus and the glens with your own car.

SIGHTS & ATTRACTIONS

Captain Scott & Dr Wilson Cairn

This modest monument at the foot of the glen commemorates
Robert Falcon Scott and Dr Edward Wilson, who died with
Scott on his ill-fated Antarctic expedition in 1912. Wilson
lived nearby. ⓐ Signposted 1.5 km (1 mile) from Dykehead,
Glen Prosen

Glamis Castle

Childhood home of the late Queen Mother, Glamis is one of
the most impressive aristocratic homes in Scotland.
ⓐ Glamis ⓣ 01307 840 393 ⓦ www.glamis-castle.co.uk
ⓔ enquiries@glamis-castle.co.uk ⓛ 10.00–18.00 daily (Mar–Oct);
10.30–16.30 daily (Nov–Dec) ⓝ Bus: 22D (from Dundee)
ⓘ Admission charge

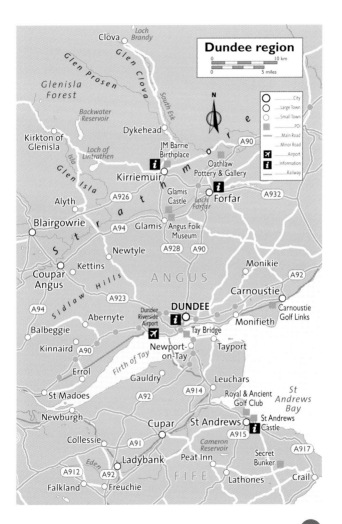

JM Barrie Birthplace

The creator of Peter Pan was born in this modest weaver's cottage, where a statue of the scourge of the pirates now stands in the garden. You can visit the family washhouse that the young Barrie used as a play-theatre. Inside, the house is preserved as it was during his childhood years here.

ⓐ 9 Brechin Road, Kirriemuir ⓣ 0844 493 2142 ⓦ www.nts. org.uk ⓔ houseofdun@nts.org.uk ⓛ 11.00–17.00 daily (July–Aug); 12.00–17.00 Sat–Wed (Apr–June, Sept & Oct) ⓝ Bus: 22D (from Dundee) ⓘ Admission charge

Loch Brandy

Hemmed in by steep hillsides above the hamlet of Clova, Loch Brandy is the perfect destination for a breath of fresh mountain air. Allow three hours to walk up to the loch and back from the car park at Clova (along well-maintained steps and walkways), or a full day to walk around the circuit of hills above the loch.

ⓐ Clova, 24 km (15 miles) north of Dykehead

CULTURE

Angus Folk Museum

This excellent little museum housed in a row of historic cottages recreates the lifestyle of rural Angus farming folk of only a few generations ago. ⓐ Kirkwynd, Glamis ⓣ 01307 840 288 ⓦ www.nts.org.uk ⓛ 12.00–17.00 daily (June–Aug); 12.00–17.00 Sat & Sun (Apr–June, Sept & Oct) ⓝ Bus: 22D (from Dundee) ⓘ Admission charge

RETAIL THERAPY

Oathlaw Pottery & Gallery

It is well worth making a short detour on the way to Kirriemuir or Glamis for a look at this gallery's attractive contemporary stoneware, paintings and glassware. ⓐ Oathlaw, near Forfar ⓣ 01307 850 272 ⓦ www.oathlawpotteryandgallery.com ⓔ ian.i.kinnear@btInternet.com

TAKING A BREAK

Visocchi's £ Formerly the sister café of Visocchi's in Broughty Ferry, the new owners have maintained the high standard of ice cream and traditional fare. ⓐ 37 High Street, Kirriemuir ⓣ 01575 572 115 ⓛ 09.00–19.00 Mon–Sat, 12.00–17.00 Sun ⓝ Bus: 22D (from Dundee)

Glen Clova Hotel £–££ The idyllically located and very well-appointed Glen Clova Hotel serves hearty pub grub in its bar and full à la carte meals in its restaurant, and will also provide packed lunches for walkers. ⓐ Clova, 24 km (15 miles) north of Dykehead ⓣ 01575 550 350 ⓦ www.clova.com ⓔ info@clova.com

AFTER DARK

The small villages of Angus and the glens are not noted for their happening nightlife, but some local pubs (including the Glen Clova Hotel) host occasional ceilidhs and folk music sessions featuring local singers and players.

◭ *Glen Clova*

Three Bellies Brae Bar Just off Kirriemuir's High Street, this quaintly named bar has a reputation for hosting the town's liveliest traditional music sessions. ⓐ 3 Bellies Brae, Kirriemuir ⓣ 01575 574 889 ⓛ 12.00–24.00 Mon–Sat, 12.00–22.00 Sun ⓝ Bus: 22D (from Dundee)

ACCOMMODATION

Glen Clova Hotel £–££ Cosy bar, posher conservatory restaurant, hotel rooms, dormitory bunks and comfortable family-sized lodges make this hotel the perfect base for exploring Glen Clova and around. Good food. ⓐ Clova, 24 km (15 miles) north of Dykehead ⓣ 01575 550 350 ⓦ www.clova.com ⓔ info@clova.com

▶ *Dundee rail station*

PRACTICAL
information

Directory

GETTING THERE

By air

You can fly to Dundee Airport (ⓐ Riverside, Dundee ⓣ 01382 662 200 ⓦ www.hial.co.uk/dundee-airport) from London (City Airport), Birmingham and Belfast, with a flying time of around 90 minutes. There are also flights to and from Jersey in the Channel Islands during summer months.

Flybe ⓦ www.flybe.com
ScotAirways ⓦ www.scotairways.co.uk
City Jet ⓦ www.cityjet.com

By rail

The East Coast rail journey from London King's Cross to Dundee takes 6¹/₂ hours. There are at least three direct trains daily. There are also West Coast trains from London Euston that require a change of train in Glasgow. Overnight sleeper services are also available.

East Coast ⓣ 08457 225 010 ⓦ www.eastcoast.co.uk
First ScotRail ⓣ 0845 601 5929 ⓦ www.scotrail.co.uk
Virgin Trains ⓣ 08719 774 222 ⓦ www.virgintrains.co.uk

By coach

There are coach services to Dundee from all over the UK. However, for those living outside Scotland and planning a short break, rail or air travel are quicker options, and may not be much more expensive.

CityLink ☎ 0871 266 3333 ⓦ www.citylink.co.uk
Megabus ☎ 0900 160 1900 ⓦ www.megabus.com
National Express ☎ 0871 781 8178 ⓦ www.nationalexpress.com

GETTING AROUND

City and suburban bus services are operated by Travel Dundee, part of the National Express group. In general buses run between 06.00 and 23.00. A full list of all Dundee bus routes and timetables can be found on the Travel Dundee website. There is a taxi rank outside the main railway station or taxis can be booked from local cab companies.

Discovery Taxis ☎ 01382 732 111
Tay Taxis ☎ 01382 450 450
Travel Dundee ☎ 0871 200 2233 ⓦ www.traveldundee.co.uk

HEALTH, SAFETY & CRIME

Visitors to Dundee are unlikely to encounter any major health or security issues, although alcohol-fuelled scraps can break out in the city centre, especially on late Friday and Saturday nights, but they are unlikely to affect anyone who simply walks on by. Ninewells Hospital is one of the most respected in the country and has an accident and emergency department should you suffer any injuries during your stay (ⓐ Ninewells Avenue ☎ 01382 660 111). Otherwise, the NHS helpline or pharmacists in local chemists should be able to help with any minor ailments.

Ambulance, Fire, Police ☎ 999
NHS 24 Medical Advice ☎ 08454 242424
Tayside Police ⓐ West Bell Street ☎ 0300 111 222

TOILETS

There are adequate toilet facilities in the railway and bus stations, and at several city-centre locations. These normally cost 20p (pay at turnstile). Free, clean toilets can be found in museums, department stores and shopping centres. Toilet facilities in bars and pubs are, in theory, for the use of patrons only.

CHILDREN

Children are welcome in almost all restaurants and in a few bars and pubs, though not many Dundee pubs are truly child-friendly. Many cafés and other eating places offer children's menus. Visitor attractions aimed specifically at children include **Sensation** (see Dundee City Centre) and **St Andrews Aquarium** (see St Andrews). The **DCA Cinema** regularly shows the latest children's films and hosts an annual children's film festival in October. A 10-minute bus ride from the city centre, **Camperdown Country Park** (ⓐ Coupar Angus Road ⓣ 01382 431 818 ⓦ www.camperdown park.com) has a pirate-themed play area and an excellent wildlife centre with bears, arctic foxes, giant eagle owls and many more creatures from Arctic and sub-Arctic regions.

TRAVELLERS WITH DISABILITIES

Dundee caters quite well for wheelchair users, with wheelchair ramps at train and bus stations and on some streets, elevator access to shopping centres, and wheelchair-accessible taxis. However, like all of Scotland's cities, many of the attractions in and around Dundee are historic, and older buildings may not have the ability to provide access. All new sights and establishments, however, are required by law to provide wheelchair access. Capability Scotland and RADAR are organisations that can offer helpful advice on disability issues, and Holiday Care is a UK-wide source of information for travellers with disabilities.

Capability Scotland ⓐ 11 Ellersly Road, Edinburgh EH12 6HY
ⓣ 0131 337 9876 ⓦ www.capability-scotland.org.uk
Holiday Care ⓐ Shap Road Industrial Estate, Kendal, Cumbria
ⓣ 0845 124 9971 ⓦ www.holidaycare.org.uk
RADAR ⓐ 12 City Forum, 250 City Road, London EC1V 8AF
ⓣ 020 7250 3222 ⓦ www.radar.org.uk

FURTHER INFORMATION

VisitScotland Angus and Dundee is centrally located on Discovery Quay. It provides a comprehensive array of services, including an accommodation booking service, transport booking services, tickets for a variety of sights and events, a range of leaflets, guidebooks and maps, and a tasteful array of Scottish souvenirs. The helpful members of staff are happy to offer any advice that will enhance your visit. There's also a VisitScotland information office in the centre of St Andrews.

VisitScotland Angus and Dundee ⓐ Discovery Point, Discovery Quay ⓣ 01382 527 527 ⓦ www.angusanddundee.co.uk
ⓣ 09.30–17.00 Mon–Sat (Sept–June); 09.00–18.00 Mon–Sat, 10.00–16.00 Sun (July & Aug)
VisitScotland St Andrews ⓐ 70 Market Street ⓣ 01334 472 021
ⓦ www.visitscotland.com ⓣ 09.15–17.00 Mon–Sat, 11.00–16.00 Sun (Apr–June, Sept & Oct); 09.15–19.00 Mon–Sat, 10.00–17.00 Sun (July & Aug); 09.30–17.00 Mon–Sat (Nov–Mar)

ACKNOWLEDGEMENTS
The photographs in this book were taken by Paul Walters for Thomas Cook Publishing, to whom the copyright belongs.

Project editor: Tom Lee
Copy editor: Emma Haigh
Proofreaders: Penny Isaac & Richard Gilbert
Layout: Donna Pedley
Indexer: Penelope Kent

AUTHOR BIOGRAPHY
After graduating from university, Robin Gauldie became a local newspaper journalist, followed by a stint on the weekly industry publication, the *Travel Trade Gazette*. He went freelance in 1989, and has written for numerous national newspapers.

Send your thoughts to
books@thomascook.com

- Found a great bar, club, shop or must-see sight that we don't feature?
- Like to tip us off about any information that needs a little updating?
- Want to tell us what you love about this handy little guidebook and more importantly how we can make it even handier?

Then here's your chance to tell all! Send us ideas, discoveries and recommendations today and then look out for your valuable input in the next edition of this title.

Email the above address (stating the title) or write to:
pocket guides Series Editor, Thomas Cook Publishing, PO Box 227, Coningsby Road, Peterborough PE3 8SB, UK.